SCHIRMER'S LIBRARY
OF MUSICAL CLASSICS

Vol. 910

FRANZ LISZT

Années de Pèlerinage

1re ANNÉE

"SUISSE"

Suite

For the Piano

Edited and Revised by

RAFAEL JOSEFFY

ISBN 0-634-00042-X

G. SCHIRMER, *Inc.*

DISTRIBUTED BY

 HAL•LEONARD®
CORPORATION

7777 W. BLUEMOUND RD. P.O. BOX 13819 MILWAUKEE, WI 53213

CONCERNING ROMANTIC EXPRESSION AND THE RANZ–DES–VACHES

THE romanesque fascinates lively and florid imaginations; the romantic is enough for deep and thoughtful souls of true sensibility. Nature abounds in romantic effects where countries are simple: long-continued cultivation destroys them in ancient lands, especially on the plains where man easily becomes full master.

Romantic effects are the accents of a primitive tongue, not known to all men, which becomes in a good many countries a foreign language. He that no longer lives with them soon ceases to understand them; yet this romantic harmony is all that preserves in our heart the color of youth and the freshness of life. The lover of society no longer feels these effects, for they are too far removed from his mode of living. He says at last: "What are they to me?" Like unto those constitutions dried up by fire that withers with slow and constant poison, he finds himself old in the prime of life; although he has the outward appearance of a man, his life is without spring and elasticity.

But you whom the great crowd regards as one of it, because you live simply, because you have genius without pretensions to intellect, or simply because it sees you live, and since you also eat and sleep, primitive men, thrown here and there in the futile century, to preserve the plan of natural things,—you recognize and understand yourselves in a language which the crowd does not know, when October's sun shines through the mist on forests of yellow; when at the going down of the moon a slender stream glides and falls in a meadow inclosed with trees; when under a summer sky and in a cloudless day a woman's voice sings in the afternoon, at some little distance, in the midst of the walls and the roofs of a great city.

Imagine a sheet of clear white water. It is large but bounded. Its oblong form—somewhat circular—stretches towards the wintry west. High summits, majestic oaks, inclose it on all sides. You sit on the slope of the mountain above the northern strand which waves cover and unbare. Perpendicular crags are behind you and ascend to the home of the clouds; the bitter polar wind has never blown over this happy bank. On your left the mountains part; a peaceful valley lies in their depths; a torrent rushes down from the snowy heights that shut it in; and when the morning sun appears between their icy teeth, through the mists, when voices on the mountain reveal the châlets above the meadows still in the shade, a primitive world awakens; there is the monument of our unknown destinies.

Lo, the first nocturnal moments, the hour of rest and sublime sadness. The valley is smoky, it begins to grow dark. The lake toward the south is already in the night; the huge cliffs that inclose it are a sombre zone beneath the frozen dome which rises above them and seems to set in its frosts the light of day. The last fires of the sun yellow the many chestnut trees on the savage rocks; they pass in long rays under the lofty darts of the Alpine firs; they tinge with brown the mountains; they light up the snowbanks; they kiss the winds. The unruffled water, brilliant with light and blended with the sky, is now as limitless as the heaven, and purer, more ethereal, more beautiful; its calmness astonishes; its transparency deceives; the aerial splendor which it reflects seems to go down to its depths, and under its mountains, separated from the earth as though suspended in the air, you find at your feet the emptiness of the sky and the immensity of the world. It is now the hour of fascination and forgetfulness. You no longer know where are the mountains and where the sky, nor on what you yourself are resting; you no longer find a plane, there is no longer a horizon; there are new ideas, unknown sensations; you have left the life of every day. And when this vale of water is all in shadow; when the eye no longer discerns objects or measures distances; when the evening breeze has stirred the waves, then, toward the west, only the very end of the lake remains illuminated with a pale light; everything inclosed by the mountains is only an indistinguishable gulf, and in the midst of the shadows and the silence you hear, a thousand feet below, the restless, ever recurring billows, which come and go without ceasing, shudder at regular intervals on the strand, pour into the recesses of the cliffs, break on the bank; and their romantic clamor resounds in a long murmuring in the unseen abyss.

Nature has put the most forcible expression of romantic character in sounds, and it is especially by the sense of hearing that you can render perceptible by a few impressions and in a striking manner both extraordinary places and things. Odors provoke quick perceptions, huge but vague. That which is perceived by the eyes seems to interest the mind rather than the heart. You admire what you see; but you feel what you hear. The voice of a loved woman will be even more beautiful than her features; the sounds heard in sublime regions will make a deeper and more abiding impression than that gained through the visual appearance of the same places. I have seen no picture of the Alps which made them as real to me as when they are recalled by a melody that is truly Alpine.

The ranz-des-vaches not only calls memories to the mind, it paints. I know Rousseau has spoken in a contrary manner, but I believe he deceived himself. This effect is not imaginary. Two persons looking separately at the plates of "Tableau pittoresque de la Suisse" said in turn on seeing the Grimsel: "That is the place to hear the ranz-des-vaches." If the ranz-des-vaches is played faithfully rather than with mere skill, if the player really feels the music, the first notes take you to the high valleys, near rocks that are bare and near those that are of a reddish gray, under a cold sky and a burning sun. You are on the ridge of heights that are rounded and abound in pasturage. You are deeply conscious of the slowness of things, of the grandeur of places. You find there the quiet walk of the cows and the measured swing of their large bells, near the clouds in the stretch that gently slopes from the crest of deep-rooted granite even to the granite of snowy ravines. The winds rustle chill in the distant larches. You hear the roaring of the torrent hidden in precipices which it has dug out in the course of centuries. These sounds, solitary in space, are followed by the hasty, heavy accents of the ranz-des-vaches, the wandering expression of a pleasure without merriment, of the joy of the mountains. The songs are at an end; man leaves the scene; the bells have gone by the larches; only the shock of rolling stones is heard, the interrupted fall of trees which the torrent pushes toward the valleys. The wind brings forward or withdraws these Alpine sounds. When they are wholly lost, all seems cold, motionless, dead. It is the domain of the man who regards nothing; he leaves his cottage, large or humble, which heavy stones insure against the storm; he knows not whether the sun burns, the wind howls, or the thunder roars beneath his feet. He walks on the side where the herd should be, and the cows are there; he calls to them, they come together, in turn they near him, and he goes back slowly as he came, laden with the milk for the plains which he will not know. The cows stand still and chew the cud. There is no longer any visible movement. Man has disappeared. The air is cold; the wind died with the evening light; there is only the glimmer of ancient snowbanks, only the plunge of torrents whose wild murmur arising from the depths adds, as it seems, to the lasting silence of lofty summits, glaciers, and the night. They say that one of these bucolics, composed in Appenzell, and in German, ends about as follows: "Profound shelters, quiet forgetfulness! O peace of men and of regions; O peace of valleys and lakes! Free shepherds, hidden and unknown families, simple customs! Give to our hearts the calm of the châlet and renunciation under the rude sky. Wild mountains! Chill refuge! Last resting-place for a simple, independent soul."

DE SENANCOURT'S "OBERMANN."

THE RANZ DES VACHES

THE ranz des vaches is an air sung or played by Swiss mountain cowherds. There has been much dispute concerning the origin of the term. The term probably came from the German Kuhreigen or Kuhreihen, which may be translated into English, "cowbrawl." Littré says the French term originated in the canton of Freiburg. Tarenne says : "*Ranz des vaches*, for *Rang des vaches*, should mean 'the walk of the cows,' or the air sung by Swiss cowherds when the cows go, one after the other, through a mountain pass. This definition is probably correct, for the cows are all named in the oldest ranz, especially in that of Appenzel." Some have thought that the words of the songs, different in the various cantons, were set to old Alphorn tunes. The Alphorn is a primitive, very old instrument, a trumpet in the form of a *cornet à bouquin*, or of a cow's horn. It was possibly at the beginning the horn of a cow. The ordinary length of the Alphorn is six feet. The Swiss make the instrument out of the bark of a slender tree. The bark is rolled as though it were pasteboard, and a mouthpiece of hard wood is inserted. Packthread is wound about the tube to keep it firm. The influence of the ranz des vaches on the homesick Swiss in foreign lands is traditional; and one of these airs, the one perhaps the most familiar and not unlike the theme chosen by Liszt, was published in Hoffer's (Théodore Zwinger's) "Dissertation sur la Nostalgie" (Basle, 1710). The tune given in Rousseau's "Dictionnaire de Musique" was changed by the writer. The collection entitled "Acht schweizer Kühreihen, mit Musik und Text," and published at Berne nearly a century ago, is said to be inaccurate and uninteresting. Viotti, the violinist, noted an Alphorn melody heard by him at sunset. His account of it, with the tune, is to be found in the "Décade philosophique" (An. 6). Rousseau's perverted air was used by Grétry in his overture to "Guillaume Tell" (1792), and Adam also used it in his "Méthode de piano du Conservatoire." One of the most effective employments of an Alphorn tune is by Alexis Chauvet (1837-1871), a page in a collection of short piano pieces ("Album Leaves"), some of which were orchestrated by Henri Maréchal. George Tarenne's "Recherches sur les Ranz des Vaches" (Paris, 1813) contains several Alphorn tunes with words sung in cantons at that time, and it also contains much miscellaneous and curious information. For an interesting note on the influence of the Alphorn on modern Swiss music, see E. Ansermet's "La Musique en Suisse" published in "Le Mercure Musical" (Paris) of June 15, 1906, pp. 574-5.

[PHILIP HALE.]

WHAT do I wish? What am I? What shall I ask of nature?—Every cause is invisible, every end is deceitful; all forms change, all lengths of duration finally come to an end. ...I feel; I exist only to waste myself in unconquerable longings, to drink of the seduction of a fantastical world, to remain a subject to its voluptuous illusion. "OBERMANN": LETTER 53.

INEXPRESSIBLE sensibility, the charm and the torment of our futile years; vast consciousness of a nature that is everywhere incomprehensible and overwhelming; universal passion, indifference, the higher wisdom, abandonment to pleasure—all needs and profound and tedious cares that the heart of man can know; I have felt and experienced them all on that memorable night. I have made a sinister step toward the period of feebleness. I have consumed ten years of my life. "OBERMANN": LETTER 4.

COULD I embody and unbosom now
That which is most within me,—could I wreak
My thoughts upon expression, and thus throw
Soul, heart, mind, passions, feelings, strong or weak,
All that I would have sought, and all I seek,
Bear, know, feel, and yet breathe,—into *one* word,
And that one word were Lightning, I would speak:
But as it is, I live and die unheard,
With a most voiceless thought, sheathing it as a sword.

BYRON: "CHILDE HAROLD," III. xcvii.

ÉTIENNE Pivert de Senancourt was born in Paris in 1770. He died in St.-Cloud, Jan. 10, 1846. He was educated for the priesthood, but he did not wish to be a priest, and he ran away from home and lived at Freiburg, Switzerland. There he married (his wife died about 1800) and as an *émigré* he returned to Paris, where he lived alone and humbly as a hack-writer. The death of his wife and extreme poverty enlarged his natural melancholy. A small pension was granted to him in 1830. "Obermann," a romance, the story of a solitary and depressed person, skeptical and tired of life, told in a series of letters written from Switzerland, was published in 1804, but it did not attract attention until about 1830. Senancourt wrote a sequel, "Isabelle," which was published at Paris in 1833. Among the other works of Senancourt are "Rêveries sur la Nature primitive de l'Homme" (1799), "Libres Méditations d'un Solitaire inconnu," and "l'Amour selon des Lois primordiales" (1805). Influenced in a measure by Rousseau and Chateaubriand he was a writer of marked originality both in thought and expression. Matthew Arnold's admiration for him is well known, and it found vent to those who know the poet rather than the essayist in "Stanzas in Memory of the Author of 'Obermann,' Nov., 1849," which begin:

In front the awful Alpine track
Crawls up its rocky stair;

and in "'Obermann' Once More." Senancourt wished this line for his epitaph: "*Éternité, deviens mon asile!*" His daughter Pauline wrote several novels.

George Sand wrote an essay in 1833 on "Obermann" in which she studied the peculiar melancholy of Senancourt and compared his disillusionized hero with Goethe's Werther and Chateaubriand's René. This essay was republished in her "Questions d'Art et de Littérature" (Paris, 1878). See also the essay of Sainte-Beuve, "Portraits contemporains" (vol. i. pp. 143, 173, Paris, 1891); "Un Précurseur," by J. Lavallois (Paris, 1867); and A. E. Waite's "Obermann" (London, 1903). [PHILIP HALE.]

CONTENTS

PAGE

1. CHAPELLE DE GUILLAUME TELL 2

2. AU LAC DE WALLENSTADT 9

3. PASTORALE 13

4. AU BORD D'UNE SOURCE 17

5. ORAGE 25

6. VALLÉE D'OBERMANN 35

7. ÉGLOGUE 50

8. LE MAL DU PAYS 54

9. LES CLOCHES DE GENÈVE. Nocturne 57

19296

Années de Pèlerinage

Années de Pèlerinage
I
Chapelle de Guillaume Tell

Edited and revised by
Rafael Joseffy

Franz Liszt

19296 r

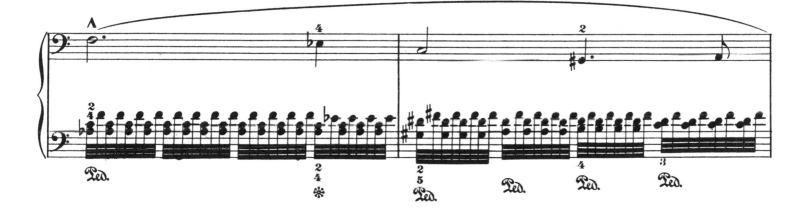

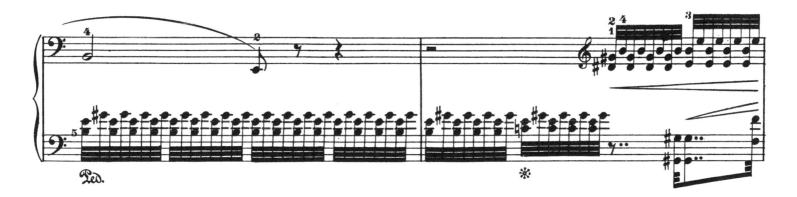

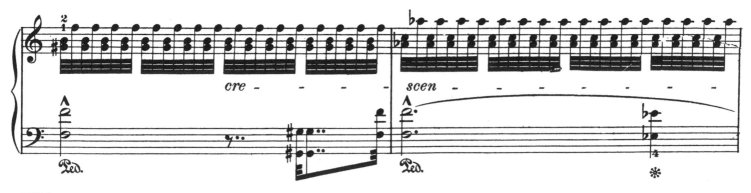

19296

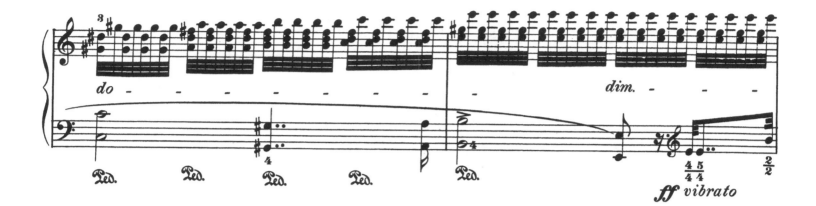

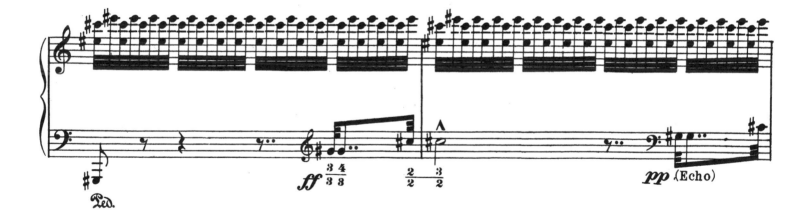

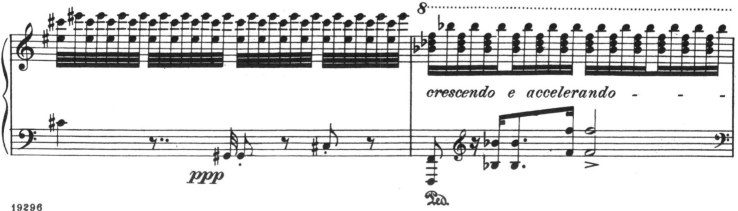

Allegro vivace

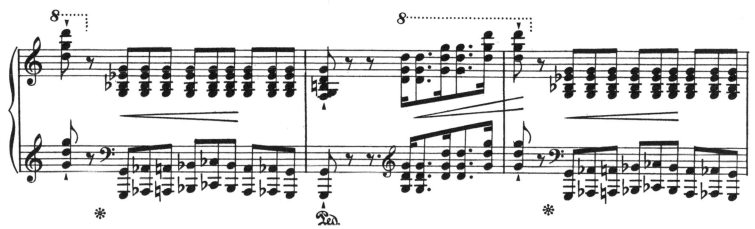

Più moderato

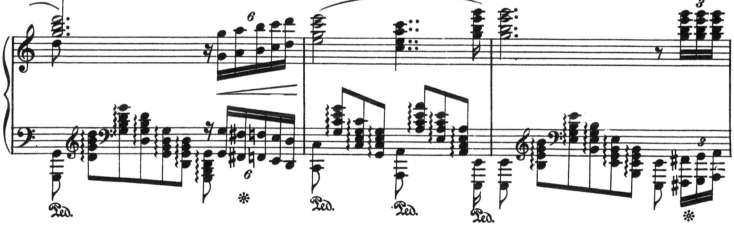

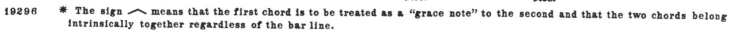

7

largamente
meno forte

rinforz.

rinforz.

espressivo

19296   ✳ The sign ⌢ means that the first chord is to be treated as a "grace note" to the second and that the two chords belong
intrinsically together regardless of the bar line.

Années de Pèlerinage
II
Au lac de Wallenstadt

Edited and revised by
Rafael Joseffy

Franz Liszt

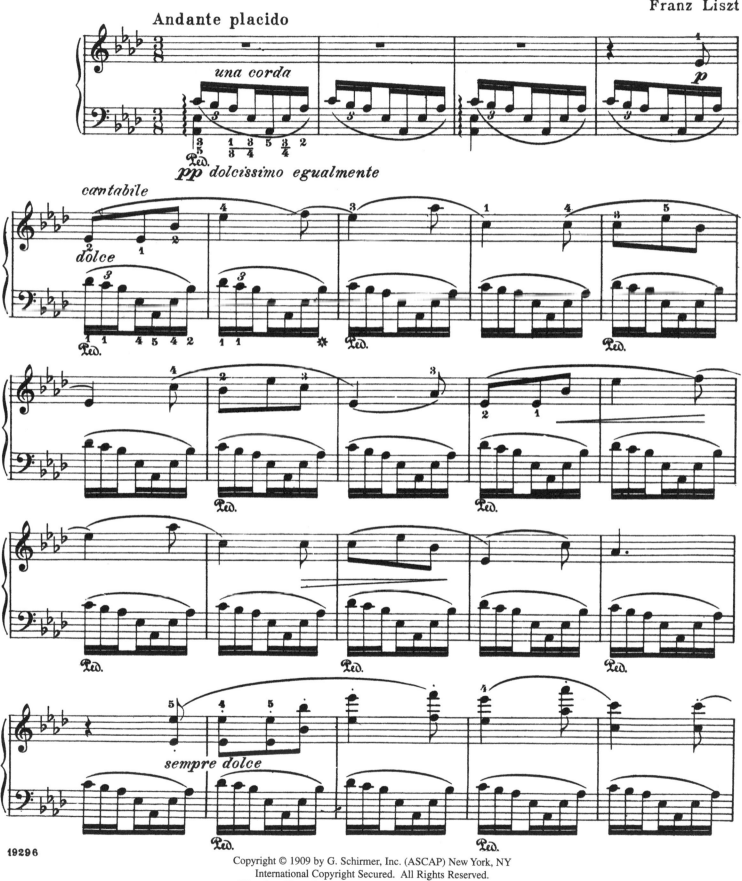

Années de Pèlerinage
III
Pastorale

Edited and revised by
Rafael Joseffy

Franz Liszt

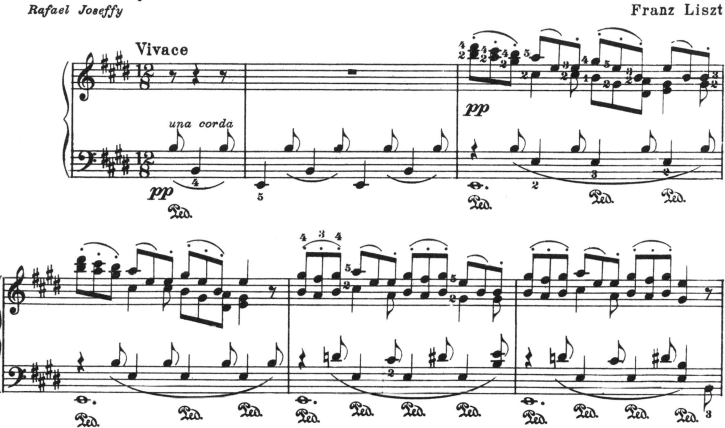

19296

un poco marcato
tre corde

senza Pedale

una corda

pp

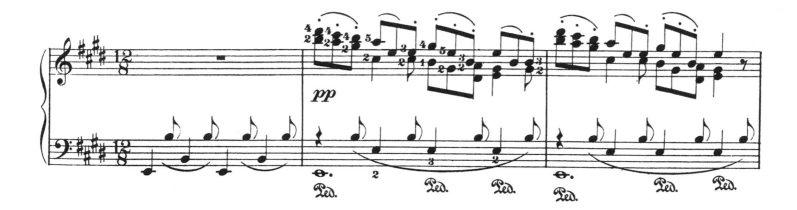

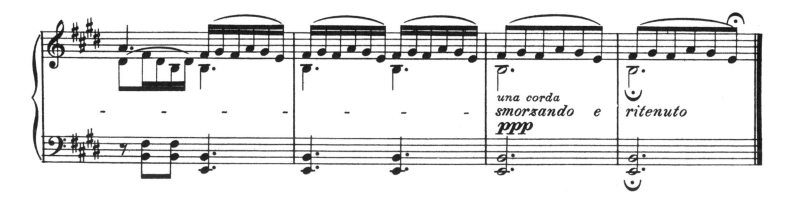

Années de Pèlerinage
IV
Au bord d'une source*

*Edited and revised by
Rafael Joseffy*

Franz Liszt

sempre dolce e grazioso

p tranquillo

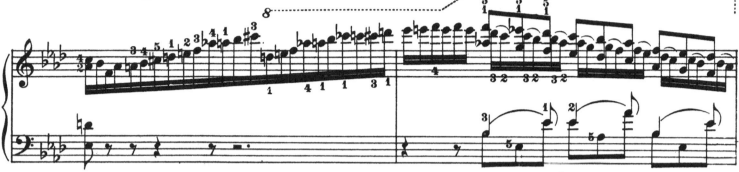

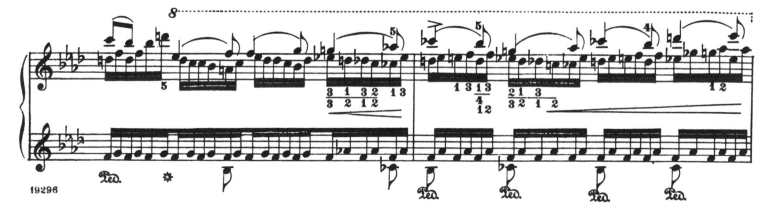

19296

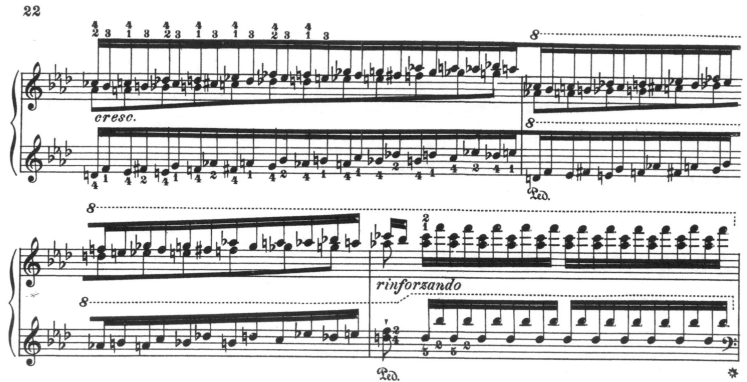

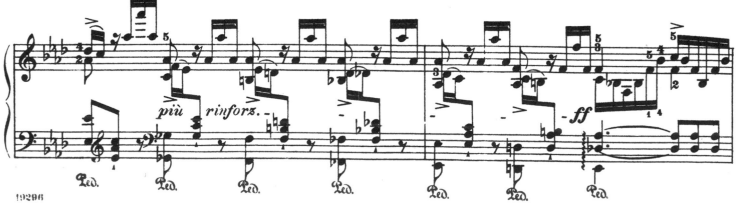

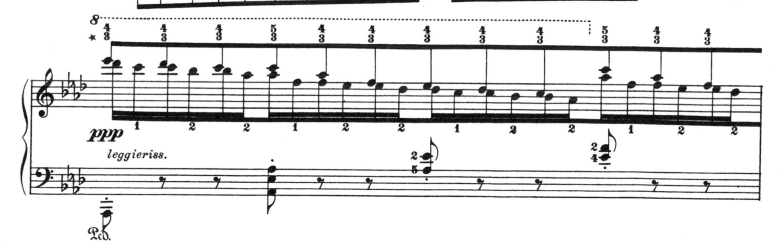

Années de Pèlerinage
V
Orage

Edited and revised by
Rafael Joseffy

Franz Liszt

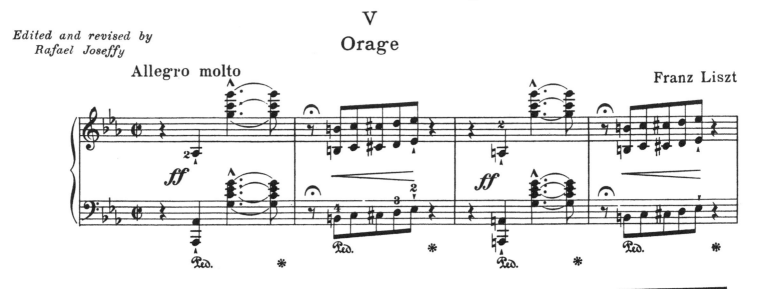

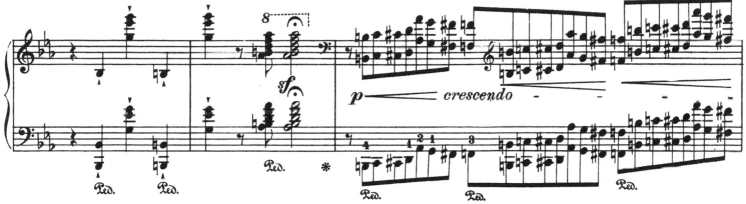

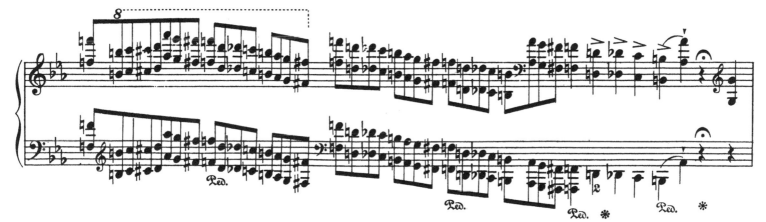

19296

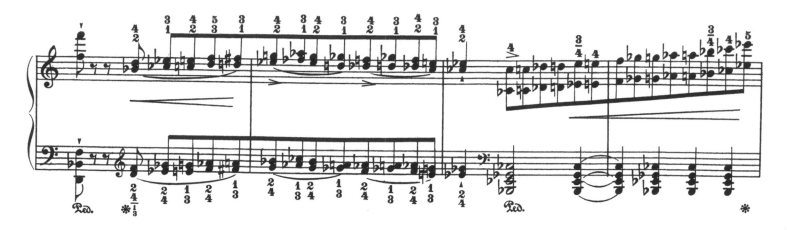

Meno allegro

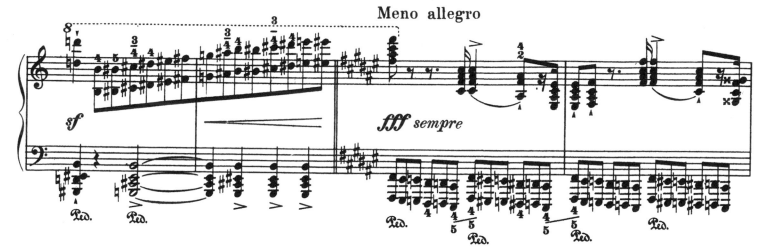

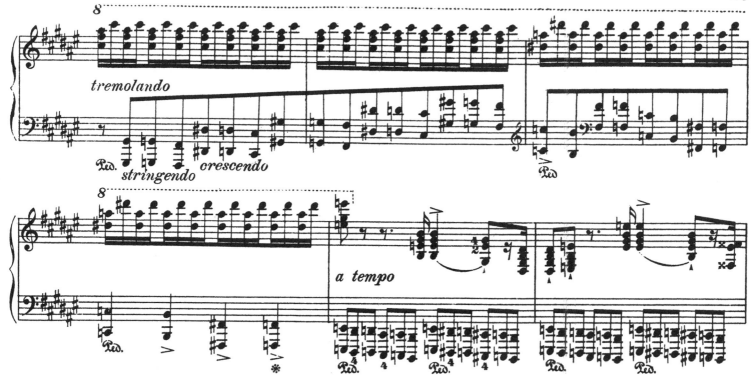

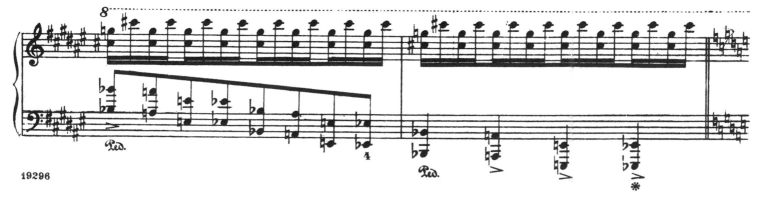

19296

Più moto

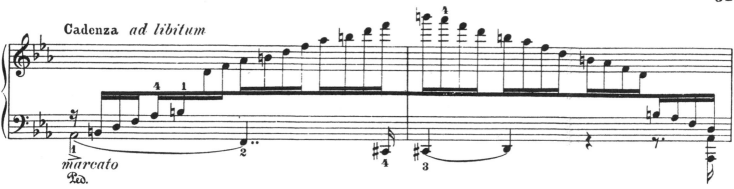

Cadenza *ad libitum*

marcato
Ped.

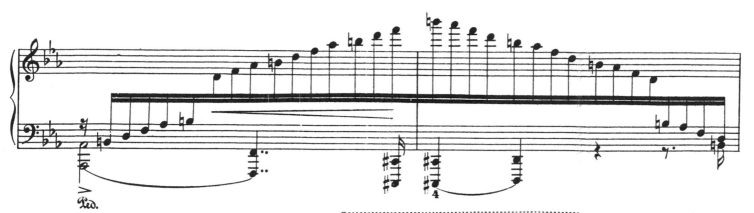

Ped.

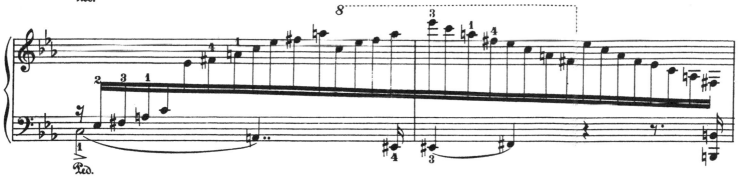

Ped.

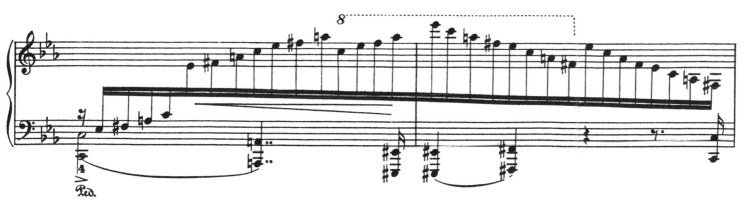

Ped.

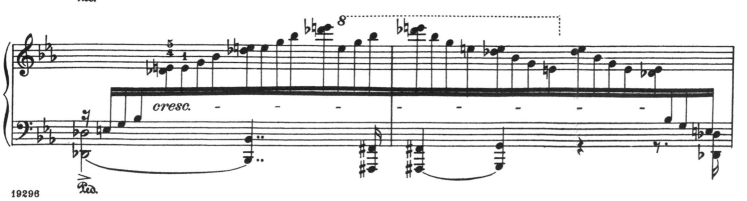

cresc.

Ped.

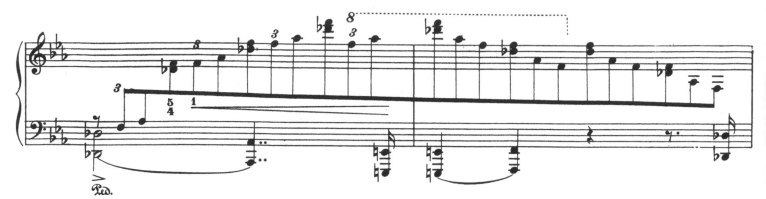

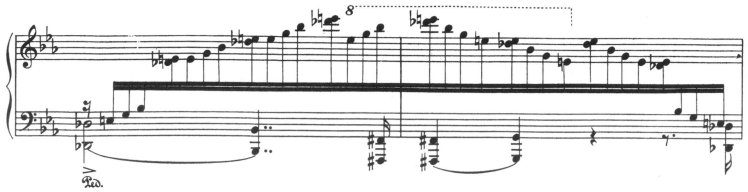

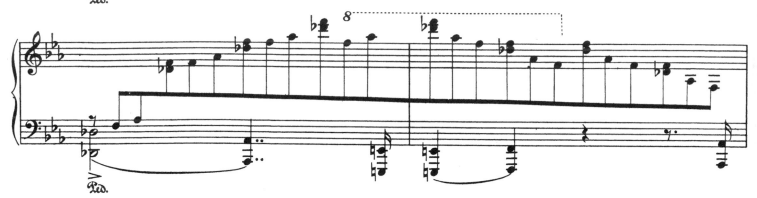

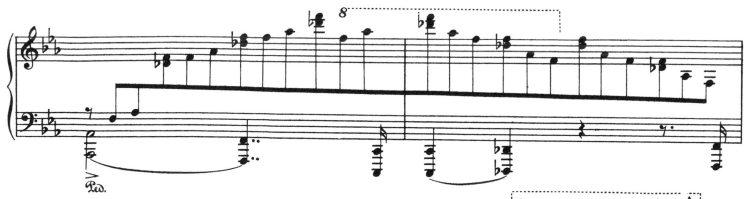

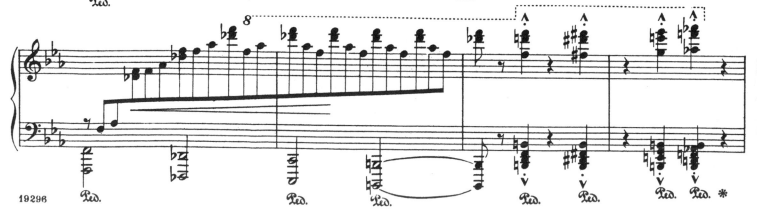

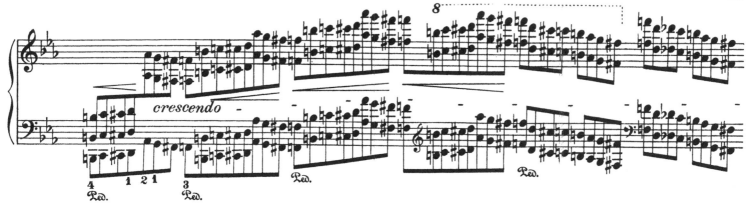

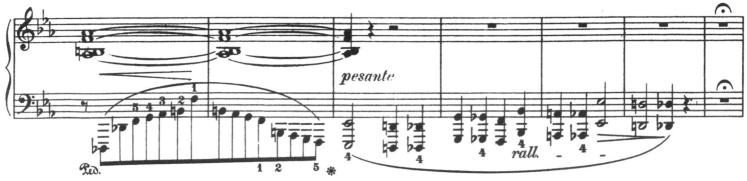

Années de Pèlerinage

VI

Vallée d'Obermann

Edited and revised by
Rafael Joseffy

Franz Liszt

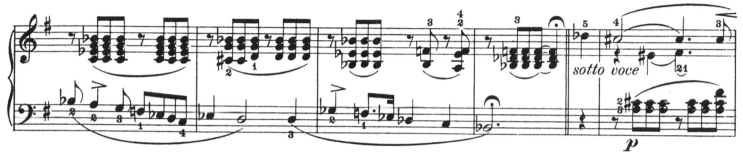

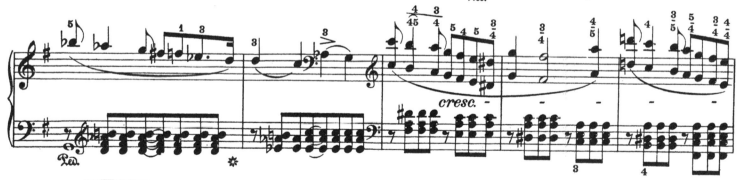

Più lento

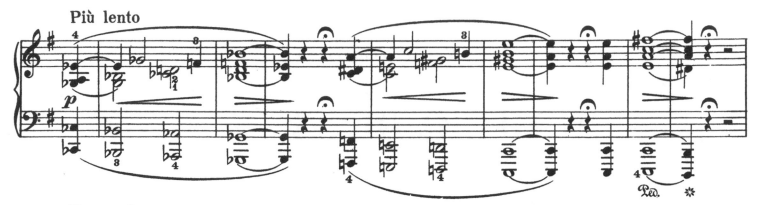

Tempo I

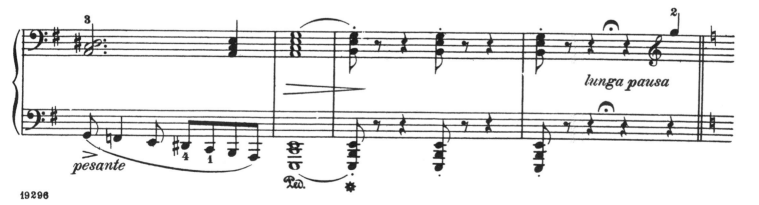

Un poco più di moto, ma sempre lento

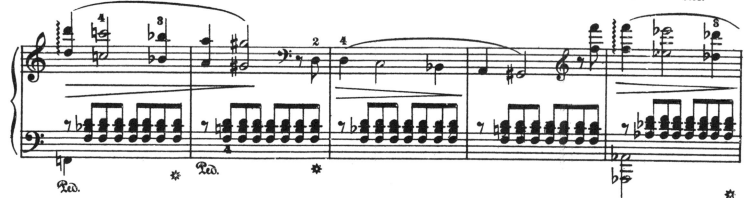

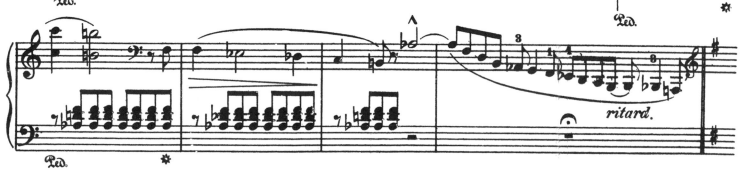

19296

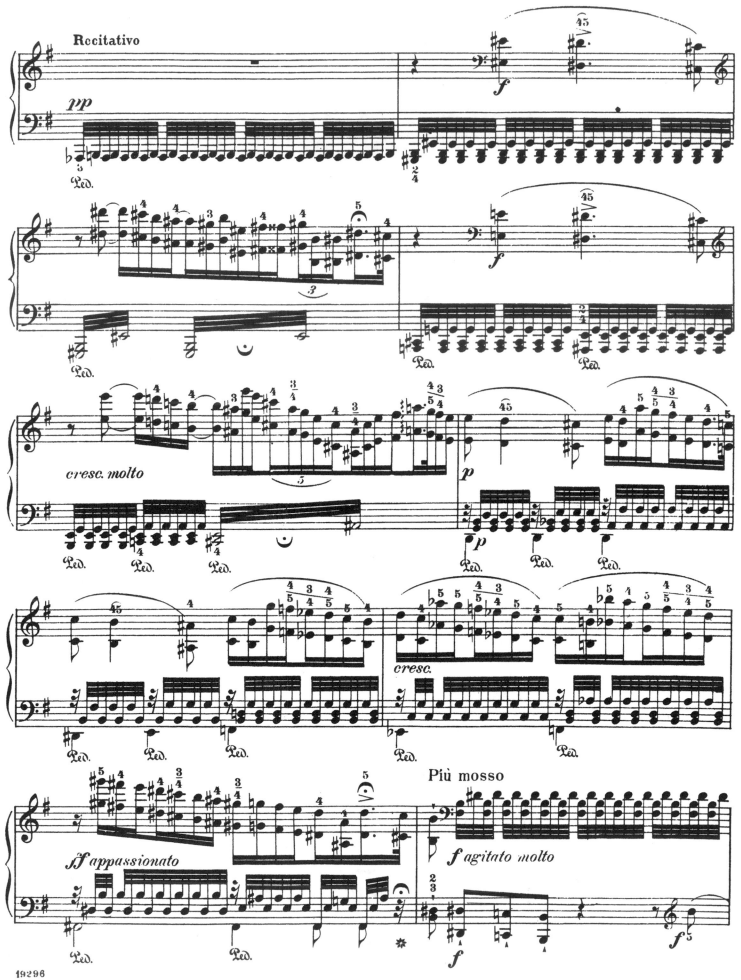

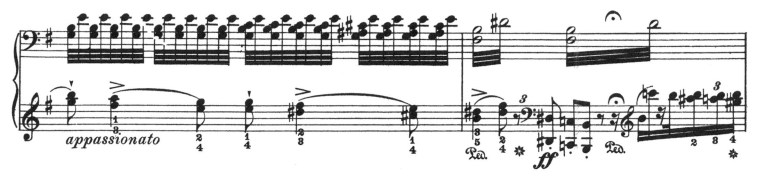

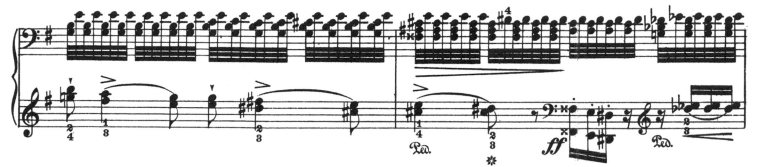

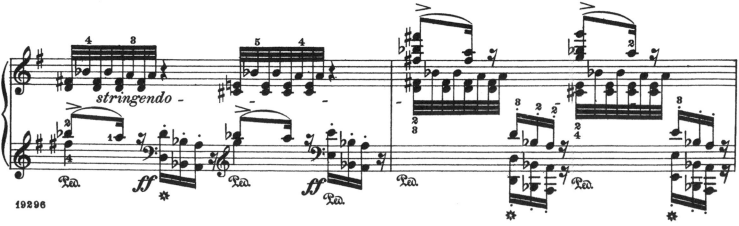

19296

Presto

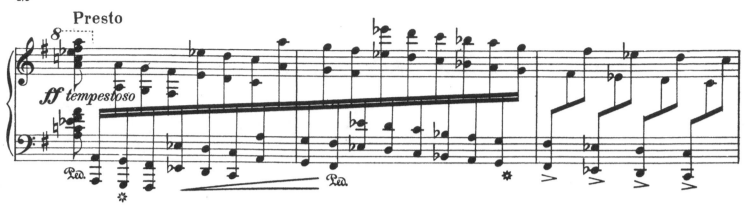

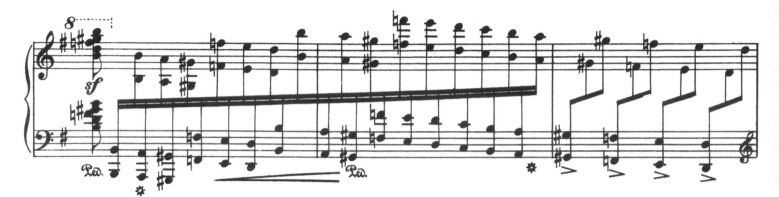

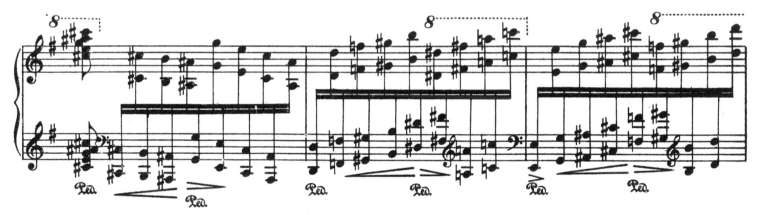

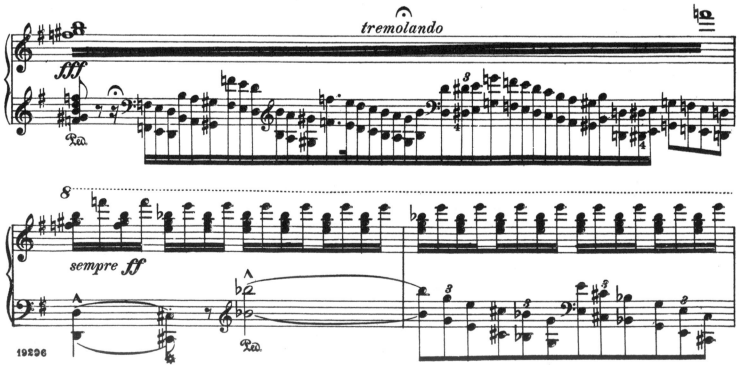

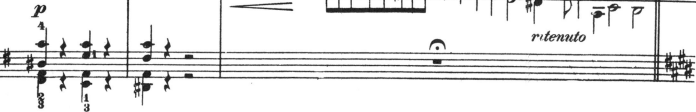

19296

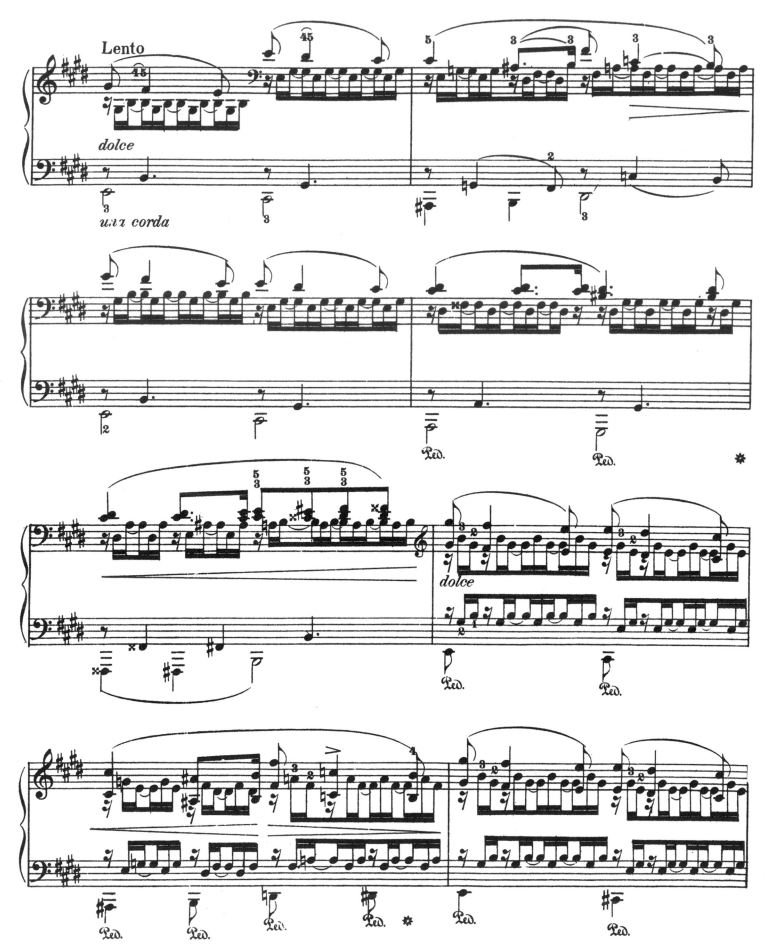

marcato espressivo

sempre animando sino al fine

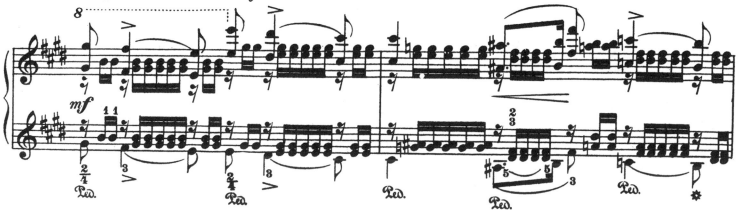

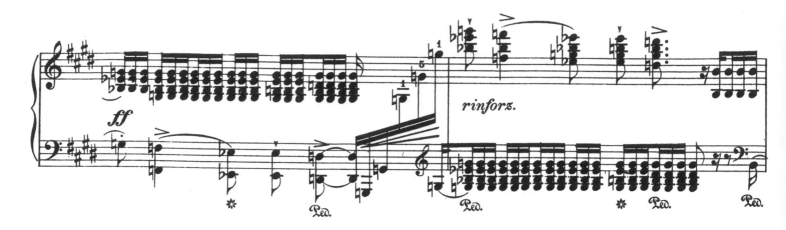

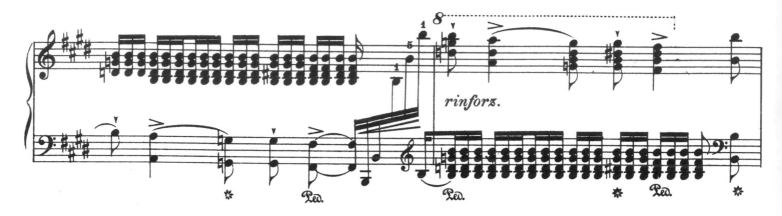

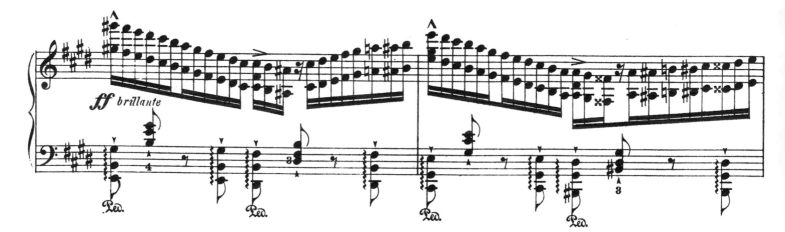

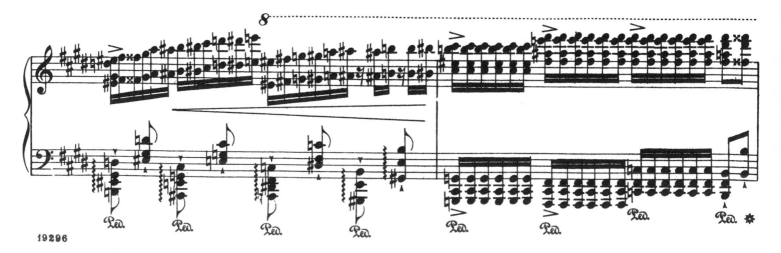

48

19296

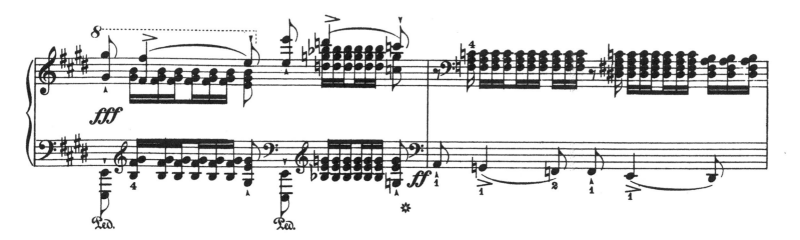

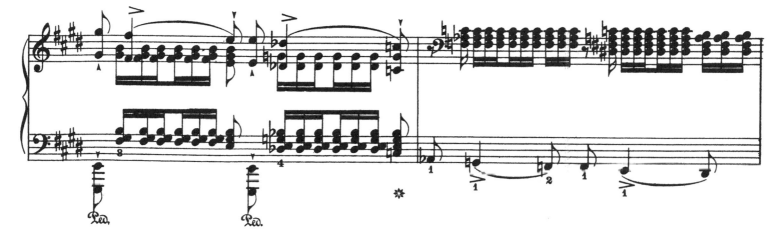

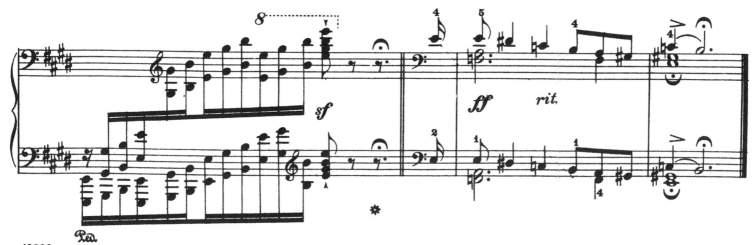

19296

Années de Pèlerinage
VII
Églogue

Edited and revised by
Rafael Joseffy

Franz Liszt

19296

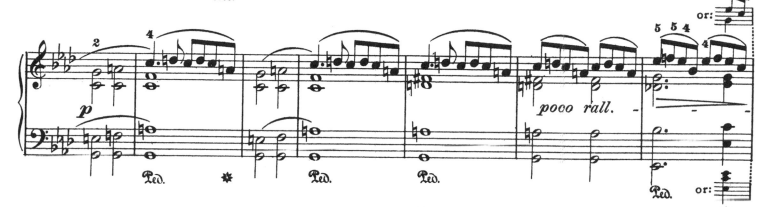

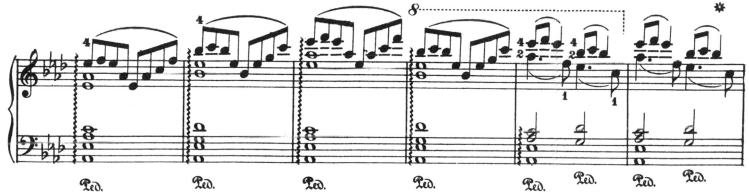

19296

Années de Pèlerinage
VIII
Le Mal du Pays

Edited and revised by
Rafael Joseffy

Franz Liszt

19296

Années de Pèlerinage
IX
Les cloches de Genève

Nocturne

Edited and revised by
Rafael Joseffy

Franz Liszt

19296

Cantabile con moto *(sempre rubato)*
la melodia accentata assai

l'accompagnamento dolce quasi arpa

dolcissimo

un poco slentando

dim. - *più dolce*

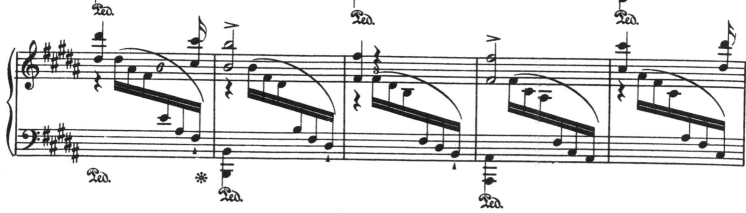

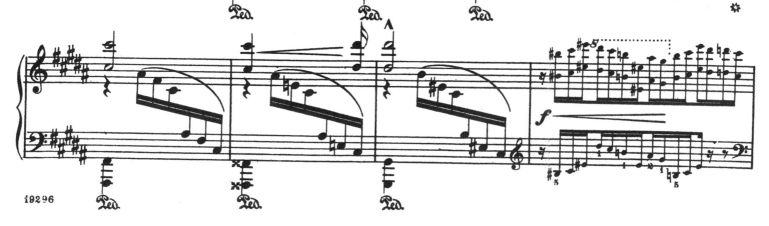

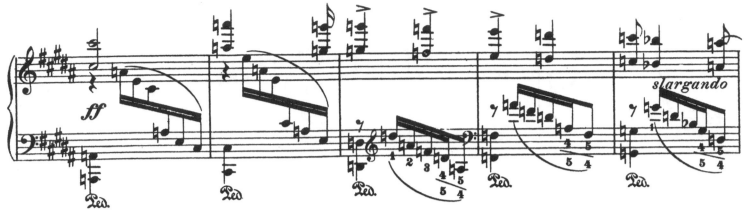

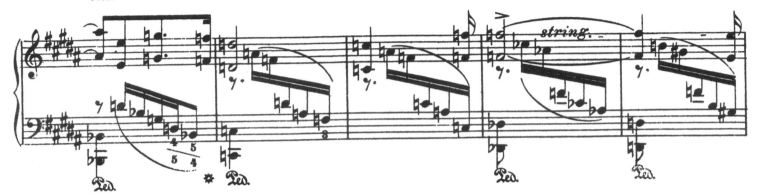

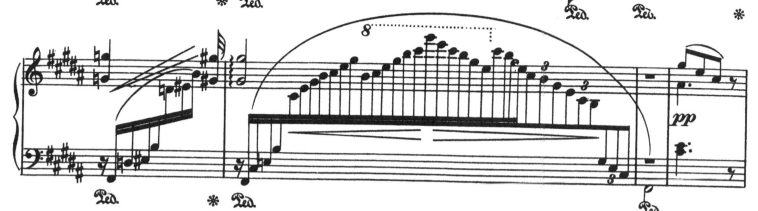

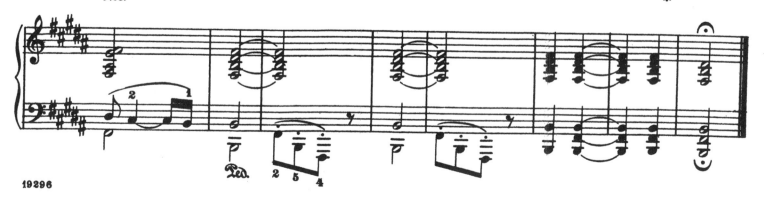

19296